Priceless Treasure

7th Chapter

AuthorHouse™ LLC
1663 Liberty Drive
Bloomington, IN 47403
www.authorhouse.com
Phone: 1-800-839-8640

Published by AuthorHouse 03/19/2014

ISBN: 978-1-4918-5405-1 (sc)
*   978-1-4918-5406-8 (e)*

Library of Congress Control Number: 2014901275

Any people depicted in stock imagery provided by Thinkstock are models,
and such images are being used for illustrative purposes only.
Certain stock imagery © Thinkstock.

Scripture quotations marked NJB are from The New Jerusalem Bible, copyright © 1985 by Darton, Longman
& Todd, Ltd. and Doubleday, a division of Random House, Inc. Reprinted by Permission.

This book is printed on acid-free paper.

FOREWORD

As parish priest of Saint Benedict's Parish, it is my pleasure to present this wonderful book to the general public written by *The 7th Chapter,* entitled "Priceless Treasure." *The 7th Chapter* group of women from Saint Benedict's Parish, Morne Fortune, Castries, Saint Lucia has embarked on a Faith Teaching Project. The focus of this work is based on teaching the essentials of the Holy Eucharist to children between ages 8 and 11 years. It is important to make mention that 5 members of this group of women are trained teachers who have taught school at various levels and ages. This book is certainly very timely and will make a profound contribution to the faith formation of our children, especially those preparing for the Sacraments of First Holy Communion and Confirmation.

The 7th Chapter group of women are very fervent in their Catholic Faith and continue to have a profound love and reverence for the Holy Eucharist. Hence, it is very noble that they have taken on this project as a significant catechetical tool to assist children in a clearer understanding and appreciation for the Holy Eucharist, especially as the Catholic Church embarks on the Year of Evangelization. We live in an era where there is a dire need for a re-catechesis on the Holy Eucharist, namely: reverence during the Holy Sacrifice of the Mass, Benediction and Adoration of the Blessed Sacrament, a deeper understanding of First Holy Communion as a Sacrament of Initiation.

Since the Holy Eucharist is a foretaste of heaven and central focus of Sacramental Life in the Catholic Church, it is quite fitting that the catechesis of this great Sacrament begins with basic instructions to children. The Gospel according to Saint Mark chapter 10, verses 13 to 16 tell us how people brought children to Jesus so that they would experience his gentle touch and blessing. Jesus so lovingly blessed them that they didn't want to leave him. I earnestly believe and pray that we, in the Catholic Church can create a similar craving in our children for Jesus in the Holy Eucharist.

This book certainly lays a foundation for others to follow and build upon, with regard to the faith formation of children on the Holy Eucharist. May the contents of this book enable parents, teachers and catechists to impart the essence and knowledge of the Holy Eucharist on the children of today.

Father Ignatius Dominic-Savio Cètoute, M.A., L.P.C.

Parish Priest / Professional Counsellor

Saint Benedict's Parish

Morne Fortune, Castries

Saint Lucia, West Indies

A Note to Readers

We wrote this book to help you to learn about the love of Jesus for you. We also wanted you to understand His work in your life as a Catholic Christian.

The discussion questions at the end were designed to help you learn more about your faith and the Eucharist. Try to answer them and if you find something difficult, ask for help from your parents or family members, your teachers, your catechists or a priest.

We would like the reading of this book to be an enjoyable experience but we also want it to help you to grow spiritually, to increase your faith and your love for the Eucharist.

This work would not have been possible without the support, assistance and guidance of a number of people. We acknowledge these persons below with deep gratitude.

Martina Augustin

Geoffrey Devaux

Fr Ignatius Cetoute

Fr. Cecil Goodman

Fr. Cleophus Joseph

Mark Hennecart

Alicia Stephen

Rosemarie Cooper CTBS

Annette Lubin–Biscette

Felicia McFarlane

Kuan Millar

Carson Millar

Janice Isaac–Flavien

Gabrielle and David Flavien

Tania and Naomi Isaac Hyman

Elritha Phillippe

Nancy Gomez

Toni Hackshaw

Joan Hyacinth

Lyndell St. Ville

Illustrations: Patrick Dujon

Photography: Mark Hennecart

Rosemarie Cooper – Catholic Television Broadcasting Service (CTBS)

Editor: Loyola Devaux

CONTENTS

CHAPTER ONE

Cedarville

On a lush green plateau seventy metres above the sea, depending on the weather, you can hear the sound of the waves washing gently or crashing wildly against the rocks on the coast. Sometimes the sea is calm and quiet and always you can see the tall mountains standing majestically against the skyline. If you listen carefully, you can hear the chirping of birds, the croaking of frogs and the keen creaking of crickets creating a harmonious symphony.

This is the agricultural community of Cedarville. Its fresh green vegetation and fruit trees make it a very peaceful and healthy environment. The Emmanuel children often spend the vacation there with their grandmother, Esther Jacob.

Now that their father, Matthew, was not at work, Christina and Samuel knew that they could not attend the Easter music camp. Money was short and they listened to their mother humming quietly as she planned and tried to make sure that they were comfortable. Last night, after night prayers, she told them that they were going to spend the Easter vacation with Grandma Esther.

Christina jumped up shouting, "Yea, Yea, Yeee." Samuel did a few cartwheels and landed painfully against the bedroom door. His mother admonished him lovingly, "You ought to know that there isn't enough space in this small room for your gymnastics. Come let me rub your leg." Samuel cuddled against his mother's chest as she gently soothed the painful leg.

Their mother was pleased that the children were happy with the news of going to Cedarville, a rural community in a small fishing village. The sea below the community was a lovely blue colour and the hillsides were a lush rich green. The vegetation was vibrant with colour and the fruit trees were laden at Easter time. Samuel loved climbing the guava and mango trees. Lying against his mother's chest, he must have been thinking about how Cedarville was always a treat, not only because it was such a beautiful healthy environment but it was the home of Grandma Esther. She disciplined him and his sister sternly but lovingly. Their favourite place was her kitchen which was always warm and inviting because Grandma Esther's cooking was excellent. Every time they were on their way to Grandma Esther's house, their taste buds began to tingle with anticipation. For both him and Christina that was reason enough to miss the summer camp.

The children knew that many things were hard since their father was made redundant. Christina kept asking her mother, "Mummy, what is redundant? Does that mean something bad about our Daddy?" Her mother always repeated the same answer, "No Christina. People are made redundant when their services are no longer needed in their place of work, usually because the company has fewer sales and is suffering from a reduced income. Those who have been made redundant then need to look for a new job."

Mummy pushed Samuel away gently, saying, "Now off you go. You and your sister start packing. I have a few chores to complete before bedtime." Samuel and Christina giggled and ran to their rooms.

A few minutes later, Samuel barged into Christina's room and jumped up on her bed. They always fought about this. Christina shouted, "Samuel, how many times do I have to tell you to knock before you enter? Please do not stand on my bed." He jumped off the bed quickly, saying softly, "I am so sorry Princess Christina. I am so excited to go to Grandma Esther for Easter holidays but Dada looks unhappy. Maybe we should not leave our parents alone." Christina replied thoughtfully, "Do not worry Sammy; they will get over it. You know Grandma Esther always says, 'When things get tough, a silent prayer is enough.' We will just have to pray and you know Grandma Esther will have us praying so often that you will start to pout. Remember that you will get to run around with Jason and what's his name." "You mean Ronnie?" Samuel asked. He stood looking at his feet thoughtfully. Somehow, his sister always managed to soothe his worries.

Christina who was ten and Samuel who was eight attended school in the city of Mille Fleur where they lived with their parents. Life to them seemed great until their father came home with the news that he no longer had a job. Some things would change so they would have to make sacrifices. Samuel wanted to know what sacrifices were. His father explained that one of the meanings of the word sacrifice was giving up something that you really liked so that you could help out in a difficult situation. "So", he continued, "giving up music camp would be a sacrifice, although you really want to go but you know that we cannot really afford it."

Ruth Emmanuel, their mother, was a tall, quiet, hardworking person. She disciplined the children quietly but sternly. Christina always said, "You just have to look at Mummy's eyes to know if you are in trouble."

Ruth's mother, Esther Jacob, was the children's grandmother. Strong and determined, she always let them know that her faith was the centre of her life and everybody respected that. You had to pray before meals; you had to go to Mass on Sundays; you had to be reverent in Church and you always had to thank God for whatever was happening in your life. Her altar light, in the far corner of her bedroom, cast eerie shadows in the room, especially at dusk, but you were never to touch that Virgin lamp. It was a lamp that served to light her children's life. Above all you had to give thanks for the gift of the Eucharist 'a precious treasure,' she always explained, 'in the life of every Catholic.' Ruth and their father, Matthew, never argued with Grandma Esther. She provided wisdom that helped them along the road and she gave them much love and a lot of great food.

After the children were asleep, their parents sat up for some time discussing the changes in their lives. They thought it a good idea to have the children spend some time with their grandmother until Matthew secured a new job.

CHAPTER 2

Grandma Esther's Happy Stomach

It was Sunday morning at Grandma Esther's home and she always let everyone know that Sunday was the Lord's Day and must be celebrated as a special day.

Grandma had awakened early in the morning, attended early Mass and was back home. She had changed into a lovely dress which her daughter and son-in-law had given her as a gift. She was now in the kitchen, in a place she loved to be, second to her small prayer room. There in the kitchen she was putting the finishing touches to the family lunch.

What pleasant aromas greeted the children and their parents as they approached Grandma's house. Christina and Samuel ran to meet their grandmother in the kitchen. Their parents and their friends, Ron and Jason, followed quickly.

At this time of the year it was a joy to be in Cedarville. There was so much to do. Gathering fruits such as mangoes, plums, cashews, fatpok and more was so much fun. Then there was sea bathing and the opportunity of helping the fishermen to reel in the catch and moor the fishing boats, and of course, Grandma Esther's excellent cooking, to crown it all! The children stood breathlessly in the kitchen watching Grandma stir the pot as she sang the hymn, "I am the Bread of Life."

Christina, pretending to faint from hunger, asked, "Grandma are we having roti and curried chicken for lunch today?" Grandma did not reply immediately as she was too absorbed in what she was doing. She just nodded. "Eh, Eh, what's with Grandma today!" Christina exclaimed.

Grandma answered, "I am so very happy! Even my stomach is happy." Christina looked quizzically at Grandma and blurted out, "Whaaaaat!!!!!!"

Then Grandma Esther spoke up. "I received Jesus at Mass this morning and every time I do, He makes my stomach very happy. Every time I attend Mass, even though my stomach feels empty, He always fills me up when I receive Him in Holy Communion."

"But Grandma," Christina replied, "Holy Communion is not food." Grandma replied "Oh yes my child, it is Holy Food. The food we eat like this roti and curry is food for our bodies, to keep us strong and healthy but Holy Communion is also food, Holy Food for our souls to make us holy and pleasing to God. Christina, we know and believe that Jesus is present in Holy Communion, the Eucharist which we receive at Mass. Jesus said it is His Body and His Blood. Remember the story of the Last Supper which Jesus had with his friends, the disciples. Look at the picture on the wall over there," Grandma said as she pointed to the picture of the Last Supper.

"Oh yes, I always like looking at that picture," smiled Christina. Grandma Esther continued, "Jesus and his friends sat at the table eating and drinking bread and wine. During the meal, He took bread, blessed and broke it and gave it to them saying, 'Take and eat; this is my Body.' Then He took the cup of wine, blessed it and gave it to them saying, 'Take and drink; this is the cup of my Blood which will be shed for the forgiveness of sins.'"

"I remember Grandma but how can the bread become the Body of Jesus and the wine his Blood?" Christina asked "My child," said Grandma, giving Christina a hug, "Jesus is God. He can do anything." Looking worried, Christina blurted out, "Grandma Esther, Grandma Esther, did you really eat flesh and drink blood today at Mass? Yuk!!"

"No, no, my darling. What we receive as Holy Communion looks like bread and tastes like bread, and looks like wine and tastes like wine. They are changed into the Body and Blood of Jesus. This change happens during Holy Mass at the Consecration when the priest says the same words Jesus said at the Last Supper,

'This is my Body; this is my Blood.' When a man becomes a priest, at his ordination, he receives the power from God to say these same words which change bread and wine into the Body and Blood of Jesus. Because we do not eat flesh and drink blood, Jesus allows the host and the wine to retain their taste when, in fact, they are no longer bread and wine but the true Body and Blood of Jesus Christ in the Eucharist."

Samuel chipped in, "Then Grandma, the priest is like Jesus. Father Paul is like Jesus. Wow, that's neat!" "Yes, all priests are like Jesus because He gives each priest, at his ordination. the power to change bread and wine into His Body and Blood."

"Now Christina, I believe you are hungry and everything is ready for lunch. Go and call the others." The family–Mum, Dad, Grandma, Christina and Samuel and their friends sat down to lunch. Unlike her chatty self, Christina was very quiet during the meal.

Later when Grandma was resting in her room, Christina tiptoed in, climbed into her bed and snuggled up to her grandmother. "Well dear, what is it?" asked Grandma. Christina hesitated. "Grandma how can a priest be like Jesus? Jesus is God and the priest is a man." Grandma sighed, "Listen to me," she said, "Jesus is God and He was also a man. While He was on earth He founded the church, our Catholic Church, but had to return to His Father in Heaven. He wanted men to take care of and carry on His church. That is why he made the apostles the first priests and gave them, and all other priests, the power to change bread and wine into the Holy Eucharist—THE BODY AND BLOOD OF JESUS CHRIST."

CHAPTER 3

Jesus' Love for Mankind

Christina and Samuel were now living with Grandma Esther in Cedarville and quite settled in their new school. One day Christina ran home to relate to her grandmother what had happened at her school. "Grandma", she exploded with excitement, "Father Paul visited our class and spoke to us about God's love. He said because God loves us He sent His only son, Jesus, into the world to save us, and that we too, must love God in return."

"Yes, my child," said Grandma "We must also love our neighbour as ourselves." Christina continued, "Father talked about some of the things Jesus did to show His love for us. As a young man, He accompanied His Mother, Mary, to a wedding feast. When the wine for the celebration ran out, at His mother's request, Jesus changed water into wine." "Yes, Christina," Grandma said. "This was Jesus' first public miracle."

"Did you know, Grandma," said Christina, "that Jesus spent the last three years on earth travelling through the countryside preaching to the people, teaching them the things they should do in order to be saved? He healed many sick persons and cured lepers. Grandma, who are lepers?" Grandma answered, "These are people who suffer with a dreadful skin disease called leprosy and because it is a contagious disease, they have to live apart from the community." Christina continued eagerly, "He made the blind see and made the lame walk and even raised the dead to life. Can you believe that Grandma?"

Christina said, " Thanks Grandma," and continued breathlessly with her account. "Father said one day a large crowd followed Jesus to an isolated place. They became hungry but there were no shops or places to buy food. However, there was a little boy with only five loaves and two fish. Jesus asked the disciples to bring Him the five loaves and two fish and let the people sit down. He then took the five loaves and two fish, raised His eyes to heaven, blessed and broke them, and gave them to the disciples to share among the people. After everyone had eaten and was satisfied, the disciples collected twelve baskets of fragments."

"Grandma," Christina continued, "Father Paul told us something which at first I found difficult to believe." "What is it, my daughter?" replied Grandma. Just then Samuel burst into the room exclaiming, "I am soooo thirsty. Is there any lime juice left Grandma?" "Not now Samuel," said Christina, "I am telling Grandma about Father Paul's visit to our class."

"Please, Christina, can I join you and Grandma? I would love to hear about Father Paul's talk." Christina was happy to have her brother in attendance and continued. "Jesus had a close friend named Lazarus, whose sisters, Mary and Martha, all loved Jesus very much. One day, when Jesus was far, far away, He learnt that Lazarus had fallen sick and died.

Jesus then left with His disciples to visit the family. They walked for four days to get to the house.

Mary and Martha were very happy to see Jesus but sad at the loss of their brother. They told Jesus that if He had been there, their brother would not have died. They began to cry and Jesus also wept. Then Jesus asked Mary and Martha to take Him to where Lazarus had been buried. They led Jesus to the tomb, followed by a large crowd which had come to sympathise with Mary and Martha. Although Jesus was told that Lazarus had been in the tomb for four days and the body would already be decaying, Jesus went close to the tomb and called out in a loud voice: 'Lazarus, come forth' (John 11:43). The crowd, with mouths wide open, watched Lazarus come from the tomb and move towards Jesus. Then Jesus asked them to unwrap him."

"If I had been there, I would have fainted from fright to see a dead man coming out of a tomb," said Samuel. Christina continued, "Father said many of those who witnessed this miracle loved Jesus even more and wanted to follow His teachings. However, others went to the temple authorities to tell them what had happened. They were already jealous because of the large crowd which followed Jesus so these authorities decided to get rid of Him."

Christina, with tearful eyes said, "Grandma, you know what the authorities did? They arrested Jesus, gave Him a heavy cross, made Him carry it up a rugged, stony hill, laid the cross on the ground, stretched His hands out and nailed them to the cross. His feet also were nailed to the cross. Then the cross was raised up and Jesus died on it. Grandma, I do not like these people." Then Christina started to cry.

Grandma embraced her grandaughter, wiped her tears and tried to comfort her. She too wiped the tears from her own eyes. Samuel also looked sad as he recalled the excruciating pain that he felt when he stepped on that rosebush thorn behind Grandma's house two weeks ago while playing hide and seek with the boys. 'What pain Jesus must have felt having those nails driven through his hands and feet,' he thought. Grandma explained to Christina and Samuel that although Jesus was God, He came to earth and took our human nature to suffer and die for our sins because He loved us, so that He could re-unite us with His Father in heaven. Because He loved us, He did not want to leave us as orphans. He wanted to be always with us.

Grandma continued, "That night, before He was put to death, Jesus had His Last Supper with His disciples. He wanted to say goodbye to those He loved and who loved Him. Whilst they were at supper, Jesus stood up, took a loaf of bread, blessed and broke it and gave it to His disciples saying: 'This is my Body.' Then He took the cup of wine, raised His eyes to heaven, blessed it and then passed it on to His disciples saying: 'This is my Blood of the new and everlasting Covenant which will be shed for you and for all mankind, for the forgiveness of their sins. Do this in memory of Me' (Luke 22 7-34). That is why we should be reverent and attentive at Holy Mass, especially during the Consecration. Whenever we receive Holy Communion, we are receiving Jesus in our hearts. We can talk to Him anytime and tell Him all about ourselves."

"So Grandma Esther," echoed Samuel, "that is why you are always so happy whenever you receive Holy Communion? Jesus is in your heart?"

"Yes, my son, I can feel His presence because I know He is always with me, especially after I receive Him in Holy Communion."

CHAPTER 4

MINISTERS OF GOD

The children and Grandma had been to the city the previous week to attend the ordination of a young priest whom they knew. Grandma Esther would never have missed such a celebration in her beloved church. The following week, Ruth and Matthew travelled to Cedarville to see the children.

As they sat chatting, Matthew remarked. "Mom, did you see the National flag at the ordination last week?" "Come on Matthew, what does a flag have to do with the ordination?" Grandma asked impatiently.

Samuel as usual, chipped in, "Boy I was watching the flag and Jason too. So hear Jason eh, Grandma 'so many people and everybody so happy, even the flag smiling.' For true, Grandma." Grandma reflected, speaking it would seem, to herself. "My, my, it was really a joyful occasion but a very serious one. A young man was ordained to be a priest and you observed how other priests and bishops turned up for the occasion. Our church looked solemn with all its pomp and ceremony; that is because a marvellous event took place. And," she continued cynically. "Ki flag sa? What flag? Of all the wonderful things that took place, Matthew, tell me, the thing you noticed was the flag?"

Matthew Emmanuel did not like to argue with his mother-in-law, but this was special and he had to reply. "You see Grandma because all these things happened the National Flag was blowing gloriously in the wind and not only Jason noticed. I heard a nun behind me saying, 'Look at that, even the flag is happy." "You mean Sister Ryan?" Grandma had great regard for Sister Ryan of the Carmelite Community. She replied quietly "I see what you are saying. I really want you young children and your father to understand that that ceremony was very important. You must have heard the Bishop explain what an important step ordination is. Next Sunday when Father Paul comes to our family lunch as usual, you should ask him how he became a priest." The children always looked forward to Father Paul's visit. Aunty Miriam and her grandchildren would be there. It is always a fun-filled family event.

Soon that day came. The kitchen was busy with cooking activities. Aunty Miriam was making a dessert with golden apple chunks, a sort of golden apple pie. Grandma Esther was cooking red beans and dumplings. Her wonderful cabbage dish had a sweet aroma and there had to be rice and spinach—Daddy's favourite.

Christina wanted to know how many chickens were in the oven because she wanted to make sure that her drumstick was safe. Samuel also wanted a drumstick but Aunty Miriam's children would also request drumsticks and because they were guests, Grandma Esther would serve them first. So Christina ran into the kitchen sweetly chirping, "Grandmaaa." Grandma hastily replied, "No children in the kitchen." " Please, Grandmaaa, I just came to get the cutlery for the table." Christina softly replied.

"Hurry," Grandma said impatiently, "and by the way," she continued, "Did you check the number of places at the table?" "Yes, Grandma, I did," and because she could not resist it, she asked gently, " Grandma how many chickens are in the oven?"

"There are six drumsticks Christina. I knew your curiosity brought you to the kitchen. Make sure the table setting is perfect." "Yes Grandma," she gleefully replied as she pranced out of the kitchen, cutlery ringing noisily on the tray.

It was Samuel's turn to be chased out of the kitchen. As he stepped in, Grandma announced, "I said no children in the kitchen." Samuel smiled broadly, looked at Grandma lovingly and said, "Grandma, I just have to ask you something before lunch pleeease," he pleaded. "Speak," Grandma said sternly. Samuel replied softly, "Grandma I have to whisper in your ear."

Samuel had always admired Father Paul, and this was important to him, so he moved quickly and holding her affectionately across her shoulder quietly asked if she would allow him to sit next to Father Paul. She smiled and said, "Yes son, and please go help your sister set the table."

Father Paul arrived on time as he was always punctual. His blue car shone brightly in the midday sun. He was always neatly dressed. The children all ran out to meet him. Samuel held onto his hand and as they entered joyfully, Grandma announced that lunch was served and everyone should gather for the Grace before meals.

After Father Paul had prayed the blessing, Samuel quietly asked him whether anyone else could have said the blessing. Father Paul smiled, knocked gently on his glass and announced to everyone that he was about to answer a very important question that Samuel had asked.

"Anyone," Father Paul continued, "can give a blessing. For example, parents bless their children, and friends bless each other; children bless their parents; we are even asked to bless our enemies. However, the priestly blessing is a traditional blessing that goes far back to Old Testament times. Remember God asked Aaron to bless the people of Israel with a special blessing found in Numbers 6: 22-27. I am sure you all know it. It goes like this: 'The Lord bless you and keep you; the Lord make his face shine on you and be gracious to you; the Lord turn his face toward you and give you peace.' Similarly, the bishops and priests of our time are vessels of grace. They give us spiritual strength, following the example of Jesus Christ in the New Testament. We must always ask for God's grace in everything we do. St. Paul tells us 'Let us, then, have no fear in approaching the throne of grace to receive mercy and to find grace when we are in need of help' (Hebrews 4:16). Remember the priest represents Christ on earth. Whatever the priest blesses is blessed and whatever he consecrates is consecrated. His hands are specially anointed at his Ordination."

Christina chirped in, "Grandma told me last week about the priest representing Jesus on Earth, but what do you mean when you say that the priest has specially anointed hands?"

"You see," Father Paul continued, "anointing with oil comes from the Old Testament and it is a sign that someone is being prepared for sacred tasks. The Bishop anoints the hands of a newly ordained priest as a sign that he is being prepared for sacred duties."

Samuel interrupted, "I do not quite understand Ordination, Father. I know the priest wears special vestments; does he have a special mark on his hands?" "No Samuel," Father replied thoughtfully and slowly, "Ordination is that special moment when a man who has been studying for the priesthood, receives the sacrament of Holy Orders. You saw that a few Sundays ago at Father Tom's Ordination. We can look at that video sometime." The children had troubled expressions and the adults were very quiet. Then Father Paul smiled broadly and with his cheerful laughter said, "Let us continue our meal. I am so hungry. We can finish this conversation after lunch."

Everyone laughed and the usual mealtime chatter continued.

CHAPTER 5

The Presence of God

After lunch, Grandma and Father Paul were looking at the laden mango trees and chatting over coffee on the back porch. The children hovered around and Father Paul beckoned, "Come along you curious young people. We have to finish our conversation. Where were we?" Samuel replied, "The Ordination business Father!"

"Oh yes, I was explaining that the priest receives an anointing at ordination that prepares him for sacred tasks." "Oh yes," Christina replied. "I heard the Bishop explaining that. You know Grandma, they should make a movie with this Ordination, so we could have it at home and watch it again and again. I think the church should make lots of videos and sell them to parents. I really love my church".

"I agree Christina." Father Paul continued, "The most significant and most sacred task that a priest performs at Holy Mass is the Consecration of bread and wine. This happens after the Offertory. These are both very important parts of the Mass. Just as your birthday party is a special occasion and everyone pays attention as you make a wish, blow out your candles and cut your cake. Similarly, at the Offertory, the congregation is attentive as we offer prayers and the special gifts of bread and wine and wait for the moment of the great mystery of the Eucharist, which happens at the Consecration."

The priest raises the host and says the words: "TAKE THIS, ALL OF YOU, AND EAT OF IT, FOR THIS IS MY BODY, WHICH WILL BE GIVEN UP FOR YOU". Over the cup or the Chalice, He says: "TAKE THIS, ALL OF YOU, AND DRINK FROM IT, FOR THIS IS THE CHALICE OF MY BLOOD, THE BLOOD OF THE NEW AND ETERNAL COVENANT, WHICH WILL BE POURED OUT FOR YOU AND FOR MANY FOR THE FORGIVENESS OF SINS. DO THIS IN MEMORY OF ME."

"The priest's anointed hands are specially prepared for performing this wonderful mystery. The word mystery here means some event which we, as humans, cannot understand because it is from God. It is beyond our understanding but we accept this in faith. As the priest proclaims the words of Consecration, the bread and wine immediately become the

Body and Blood of Jesus Christ. You learnt this in your Catechism class. You must take time to think about what all this means. Do you know what the word Eucharist means? It comes from a Greek Word 'Eukaristos:' which means grateful, to give thanks. We normally refer to it as Thanksgiving. At Holy Mass we take our offerings to God, thankful that He has provided them and we thank Him for His life and His generous and beautiful gift of the Eucharist—His Body and Blood."

Aunty Miriam asked, "Tell me, Father Paul, how long have you been a priest?" "I have had ten beautiful years of service," Father Paul replied thoughtfully. "At every ordination we renew our promise to serve God as priests in His Church; you saw that at Father Tom's Ordination."

"Can I look at your hands, Father?" Samuel asked. Father Paul opened his hands and all the children looked at his smooth palms. Samuel looked pensive. "What were you looking for, Samuel?" Father Paul asked. "Your anointing Father, I thought I would be able to see it. The Bishop anointed your hands, didn't he?"

"You cannot see my anointing. We offer our lives to serve and the Bishop anoints us. We accept that anointing and we serve. Faith is very important. You have to trust the word of God always. Remember what Jesus said to the apostles at the Last Supper.

Remember that Jesus is the Divine Son of God, so the Bread and Wine are not just symbols; they are transformed into the Body and Blood of Jesus. Let your faith guide you. 'Faith can move mountains,' someone once said. Believe and all will be well. If you believe in the Real Presence, you will always be connected to Jesus. He will always be with you and He will become your personal friend. You young people are very interested in your faith and this is a very good thing. Faith in the Word of God keeps us strong in these difficult times. We must have more conversations like this, Grandma Esther," Father Paul smiled. "That means more invitations to lunch!" Grandma Esther smiled broadly; she was so proud of her family.

CHAPTER 6

Institution of the Eucharist

"Christina, yooo-hooo. Crissy, Crissy," Grandma called. "Yesss Grandma," Christina answered as she came running in. "Christina, lunch is ready so go and get the family and ask Ron and Jason, our friends from next door, to join us," said Grandma. "I have already told their Mum that they will have lunch with us today."

"Yes Grandma. I am very happy to help," Christina replied. She did as she was asked and soon everyone was at the table — all seven of them. Grandma entered the room bearing a tray of green bananas and fish. "Hummmm," Dad hummed. "How good that food smells; my stomach is rumbling already," Dad remarked. "Thanks for the compliment, Matthew," said Grandma. "Now Christina, pray the blessing before we eat. Thank you." "Yes Grandma," Christina chanted, "God is great! God is good! Let us thank Him for our food, Amen."

Then everyone got down to the business of enjoying the meal. As the family chatted quietly while they ate, Grandma Esther was thinking of a very long time ago and so she said, "As we sit here enjoying lunch, I am reminded of an event that took place in the time of Jesus." Christina giggled, "Hee Hee, what makes our lunch remind you of the time when Jesus had a lunch, Grandma? Green bananas and fish were not even invented yet."

"That's correct," Grandma, replied. "Now, let me tell you the story and it all goes back to my happy stomach. Jesus toured all the towns and villages around Judea, teaching and preaching in their synagogues about the good news of the Kingdom of God and curing all kinds of diseases."

"Wow!" Samuel interrupted. "How did Jesus get around these towns and villages?" "In those days Samuel," Grandma continued, "folks walked from place to place and Jesus did the same. Sometimes He got into a boat and once He rode a donkey." "Did Jesus go to all those places by Himself?" Jason asked.

"Jason," continued Grandma, "Jesus had many followers. There were twelve men whom He chose as His apostles who went everywhere with Him. Then there were the crowds of men, women and children who also followed Him. There were times too, when He and His apostles had to get away to the hills for some rest and peace. Then came the time for the celebration of the Passover, a very important religious feast of the Jews.

"Passover. Passover. What is Passover?" asked Christina. Ron quickly interjected, "Passover is a very special Feast Day in the life of every Jew. Families gather to pray and to celebrate with a special meal of very specific foods." "So Grandma, is that why the family gathering reminds you of that feast?" inquired Christina. "And you Ron, where did you learn about that feast? What's the name again?" Ron replied. " I learnt about Passover during my religious knowledge classes." "When next Father Paul comes for lunch," said Grandma, "I will ask him to tell us all about the Jewish celebration of Passover." The children's Dad, in agreement with Grandma's suggestion, exclaimed, "D'accord!"

Grandma Esther finally got a chance to continue her story, "Jesus, planning to celebrate the Passover because He was a Jew, sent some of his apostles to prepare the meal, and another two to bring Him a colt or a young donkey. He entered Jerusalem riding the donkey on His way to the feast but as the news spread around that Jesus was coming, crowds followed Him. The people were so excited and happy as Jesus was approaching, that they broke palm branches and spread their cloaks on the road for Jesus to pass. As the procession walked along, they chanted, (Ron and Dad also chanted): 'Hosanna in the highest. Blessed is He who comes in the name of the Lord. Hosanna in the Highest' (John 12:12-14). Jesus knew that was the last Passover meal He was to celebrate with His apostles because He was going to Jerusalem to die for all people." Christina blurted out, "I understand how our lunch reminds you of the Passover meal Jesus had. However, unlike Jesus' last meal with His apostles, this must not be our last meal. Your food is always so delicious."

"It is always a very happy occasion to prepare and eat a meal together as a family," said Grandma. "Now allow me to continue telling my story. During the meal, Jesus was sad because He knew He was leaving His friends and was about to be crucified. He got up from the table, took a bowl of water and a cloth and washed the feet of His twelve friends." Then Ruth, the children's mother, spoke up, "This is just what will happen in the next few days on Holy Thursday night. Fr. Paul will wash the feet of twelve men of the parish."

"Why this washing of feet?" asked Christina. Grandma explained, "In those days people walked everywhere and the roads were dusty so feet were always dusty. In washing the disciples' feet, Jesus wanted to teach them to be humble and to always serve one another. At this supper, many things happened. There Jesus instituted the celebration of the Eucharist. While they were eating, He took bread, blessed and broke it and giving it to His apostles, He said, 'TAKE AND EAT, THIS IS MY BODY.' Then He took the cup of wine, blessed it and gave it to them saying, 'DRINK FROM IT ALL OF YOU, FOR THIS IS MY BLOOD OF THE NEW AND ETERNAL COVENANT WHICH WILL BE SHED FOR THE FORGIVENESS OF SINS.'

Ron said with pride, "I know that prayer; it is said at the time of the Consecration, during Holy Mass." "That is correct, Ron," said Grandma. "At the time of Consecration, we believe that what looks like bread and wine becomes the Real Presence of Jesus. As we believe, our faith keeps us strong. When I attend Holy Mass, be it every day or on Sunday, I feel that I am in the presence of Jesus and at the elevation of the host, I gaze in amazement at the Body of Christ and I pray earnestly—'MY LORD AND MY GOD, I TRUST IN YOU, I LOVE YOU. FEED ME WITH THE REAL FOOD THAT STRENGTHENS ME.

WASH ME CLEAN WITH YOUR PRECIOUS BLOOD. MAKE ME WORTHY OF THE DRINK THAT WILL QUENCH MY THIRST FOR ALL TIME. HAVE MERCY ON ME AND ALL MY FAMILY AND NEIGHBOURS.' When I receive the Body and Blood, the whole of Jesus, under either species of bread and wine, I believe by faith that Jesus lives in me and He is with me and so my stomach gets very happy."

"Mum, do you say the same prayers every time you receive Jesus?" asked Ruth, the children's Mum. "Not really", said Grandma, "I talk to Jesus in whatever way I need. I speak with Him just as I would speak with a dear friend. Make Jesus your most important friend, for He promised, 'I will be with you for all time. I will never leave you, nor forsake you' (John 14:18). I say to you, my daughter, His promises are true so keep the faith. The Blessed Eucharist is a mystery of Faith and it is a never changing reality in an ever-changing world. Keep your stomach happy by receiving Him as often as possible."

CHAPTER 7

Faith

One Sunday morning after Holy Mass, Samuel and his friends, Jason and Ron, were playing volleyball in the schoolyard nearby. Soon feeling hot, tired and hungry, they headed home to Grandma's. The smell of food led them straight to the kitchen. They were just in time to hear Grandma saying to Christina, "Holy Communion is food for the soul and it makes my stomach happy."

"Please give me some of that food to make my stomach feel happy," Samuel said. "She cannot give it to you" said Christina. "She received it from the priest in the form of Holy Communion. She received Jesus this morning." Jason, who had walked in with Samuel, overheard the conversation and started to think about it. He knew that people of other religions also received Communion but he had never heard them say that they had received Jesus. Again, he wondered whether all Catholics believe that when they receive Holy Communion, they actually receive the Body and Blood of Christ. He was really puzzled but soon realized that he could find the correct answers. He would find out for himself; he would ask a priest or a catechist. He could not wait for the next Sunday when he would pay special attention at the Consecration. He wanted to understand that change of ordinary bread and wine into the Body and Blood of Jesus Christ who is God Himself.

Jason shared his thoughts with Samuel who really did not understand the mystery of Holy Communion. The two friends agreed upon a plan to get the true meaning of Holy Communion. They would each make a special effort to be attentive at Holy Mass and to listen carefully during the Consecration. They had been taught at First Communion instructions that at the Consecration, the bread and wine were changed into the Body and Blood of Christ but they had never really paid attention to what it meant.

As you can expect, the following Sunday the two friends were very attentive at Mass. They already knew that the Consecration was a very quiet time when everyone seemed to be more prayerful. At the Consecration they heard the priest say, "He took the bread, broke it and gave it to his disciples saying, 'Take this, all of you, and eat it. This is my body, which will be given up for you'" (Mark 14:22). He thought about the words he had heard and remembering that he would soon go up to receive Holy Communion, he prayed, "Thank you Lord. Thanks for your Body. Thanks for dying to save me." By the time he had said these words, the priest was about to raise the chalice and he said, "Take this all of you and drink from it. This is the cup of my Blood, the Blood of the new and everlasting covenant, which will be shed for you and for all, so that sins may be forgiven" (Matthew 14:24). Once again Samuel began to praise and thank God. He had remembered that at Catechism class, they were taught that the bread and wine were changed into the Body and Blood of Christ.

Again, Samuel remembered Grandma Esther. She had said that her stomach was happy. What she meant was that her stomach was happy because it was filled with Jesus. Jesus was with her. This is what happens to Catholics all over the world. Holy Communion unites them whenever they receive Jesus. Everyone who receives Holy Communion is joined together or united in one body which is Christ Jesus.

When the time came to receive Holy Communion, Jason and Samuel were both deep in thought. They were also very prayerful because they realized that something very special was taking place. When they returned to their seats, they were very reverent. They gave thanks and praise. They knew that Jesus was present with them and that they had something in common with all the other people who had received Holy Communion that day. They could not wait to return home to explain to the members of their families their new understanding. Of course, the boys chatted about it all the way home.

When they approached the house, they saw some young children playing outside. That meant that Aunty Miriam was visiting because she always brought her grandchildren with her. Jason and Samuel entered the house, greeted everyone and were surprised to see the chief catechist who greeted them warmly. Immediately the boys started to explain what they had discovered about Holy Communion.

The room became quiet and then Aunty Miriam said "I want to share something with you from my childhood. When I was a very young girl growing up in Joppa, some older children who could not speak English used to have instructions in Kwéyol. When they returned home, they would tell us what the priest had explained to them about Holy Communion. This is what they said: 'I Ka sam pèn, I ni gou pen. Mé I pa pyès pèn. Se Jézi Kwi mèm ki la.' My little sister, who did not understand Kwéyol too well, asked my mother to explain. She said, 'All Catholics believe that Holy Communion or the Holy Eucharist, is truly the Body and Blood of Jesus Christ so what the older children were saying was: 'It looks like bread, it tastes like bread, but it is not bread. It is Jesus Christ Himself.'"

Someone said, "This is absolutely true but I have heard people say that what they receive is only bread and wine." A big discussion followed and some people gave different views. Finally, the chief catechist, who was listening intently, raised his hand to get everyone's attention and explained. This is what he said: "Catholic priests have been especially anointed and consequently, they have the power given by the Holy Spirit to change bread and wine into the Body and Blood of Jesus Christ. That power was handed down from the disciples who received it from Jesus Christ Himself. Therefore only priests have that sacred privilege."

Another very important point the catechist made was that Jesus is present at the Consecration during Holy Mass. He is really the One who is involved in the miracle of changing bread and wine into His Body and Blood. Just as He performed miracles when He was on earth, He still performs miracles during the Consecration. This is the best time to talk to Him and ask for graces. When the catechist was finished, Jason and Samuel were very pleased and excited. They were happy to know that at Holy Communion what they receive is a special gift from Jesus; Jesus is present. That is something all Catholics must believe. Holy Communion makes us one with one another in Jesus Christ.

CHAPTER 8

Thanksgiving

The school term was almost at an end. Christina and Samuel were still at Grandma's in Cedarville. They were very happy there but missed their Mum and Dad very much though they spoke to them by phone regularly.

Yesterday, however, they got some good news. Daddy had found a new job and as soon as he was settled in it, he and Mummy would be coming to take them home. They were very excited. The school holidays would start in two weeks and then they would soon return to their home in the city and see all their old friends. Grandma Esther was happy too as her son–in–law had found a job and things would be better for the family but she was a bit sad to lose the company of her grandchildren. Grandma would soon be celebrating her 80th birthday at the end of June. She was planning a grand Thanksgiving Mass and party on that day, for family and friends, to thank God for her long life and for all the good things He was giving to her and her family.

It was the Friday before her birthday and Grandma was busy in the kitchen baking bread and cakes, making juices and cooking a number of other tasty dishes because Matthew and Ruth were coming for the weekend to celebrate with her. Ruth, however, had arrived early that morning and Matthew would follow on Saturday after work. She had come early to assist her mother with the preparation for the party and they were busy in the kitchen, working and chatting. Ruth had also brought some surprises for her Mum and the children from Aunty Hannah in St. Croix. Aunty could not come for the celebration but had sent a barrel filled with goodies for the family and a large parcel wrapped in birthday paper for Grandma. Mother and daughter enjoyed each other's company as they worked in the kitchen cooking up a storm—seasoning lots of chicken in preparation for the birthday lunch. There was a lot to be done.

The children arrived from school and were happy to see their Mum. Soon they too joined in the excitement, helping in some areas but getting in the way more often than not. On Saturday, the house was decorated. Lights were strung around the yard and everything was almost ready when their father arrived carrying another large mysterious package for Grandma.

Sunday morning was bright and sunny; everyone was up early getting ready to attend Grandma's birthday Mass. Ruth had laid out the children's clothes but when Christina appeared dressed for Holy Mass, in a mini skirt and a top with spaghetti straps, Grandma had a fit! "Christina," she shouted, "what are you wearing? You cannot wear such a dress to Holy Mass."

"But Grandma, this is what I want to wear; Aunty Hannah sent it for me," cried Christina, looking defiantly at her Grandmother and shouting, "I want to wear this dress. I like it and it is mine." Ruth, hearing the loud angry voices, rushed to the bedroom and said, "Christina this is not the dress I laid out for you." "I know but this is the one I want to wear. I like this one and I am wearing it!" replied Christina.

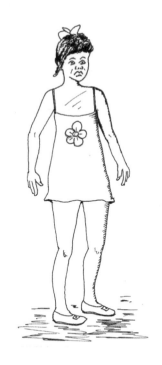

"No, you are not!" said Ruth, giving her a hug. "This is not a dress for Mass. It is a party dress. You may wear it at Grandma's party later." Christina was not very happy but Ruth was firm so she had to wear the dress her mother had chosen. Grandma was sorry that she had shouted at her granddaughter so she too gave her a big hug.

Soon everyone was ready and the family left for Mass with Grandma Esther looking very dignified in her National Dress. It was very colourful and had so many different pieces. That shiny piece around the neck, which is called the foula, was in a plain colour that matched the dress. As for the laces around the petticoat, that made her look very special. Everyone felt that the national dress was a better choice than the blue dress that Aunty Hannah had sent her and was pleased that she had decided to wear it.

During the homily, Father Paul said that the Mass was being offered especially for the life of Grandma Esther to thank God for all the years of her long life and the many blessings God had granted her and her family every day of these many years. Samuel sitting next to Grandma, noticed tears on her cheeks. "Grandma," he whispered, "are you sad?" "No, my son, these are tears of joy and thanksgiving" she whispered back. Samuel smiled.

Grandma closed her eyes again and continued thinking about her amazing life. The Eucharist had always been the centre of her life and she always thanked God for that grace. She thanked Him today for her long life and good health; for her daughter Ruth and her family, especially her lovely grandchildren Christina and Samuel; she thanked him for Matthew's new job; for her sisters, Miriam and Hannah, and all her many friends and neighbours.

At the end of the service the congregation sang 'Happy Birthday' to Grandma and Father Paul gave her a special blessing. Family and friends hugged and kissed Grandma wishing her a happy birthday. Family members and very close friends accompanied Grandma Esther home to continue the celebration. Everyone joined in setting out the food and drinks. When all was ready, Father Paul, blessed the table and said a prayer of thanksgiving for all the good food to be enjoyed and especially for Grandma's special day. The party lasted until late and everyone had a wonderful time with Grandma Esther and her family.

CHAPTER 9

FAMILY FUN

"Mummy," Christina exclaimed, "last evening was sooooo amazing. We had so much fun. The food was great, the music was lovely and everybody was happy." "Guess what Mumsie, do you know that after Holy Mass yesterday, my stomach was happy!" "Now that is interesting. How did you feel?" her mother asked. "I was singing, 'I've got a joy, joy down in my soul,' and I could not stop singing. I was so happy and I am still very happy. I think I understand what Grandma means by her 'happy stomach.' My stomach was tingling. I felt a little tickle and it was as though someone poured some syrup into my stomach. I was so happy."

"When did this all start?" her mother asked. "Well, Grandma always said, 'When things get tough, a silent prayer is enough.' I am always saying this to Samuel when he gets worried so I have been saying silent prayers for our family and as I received Jesus at Holy Communion yesterday, I realized that He was hearing me."

"So what did you pray for?" her mother asked. "I prayed that Daddy would get a job and he got one and I thanked Jesus for the celebration of Grandma's 80th birthday. I am so happy she is still strong and able to support us. When I went up to say my bidding prayers for the church, I was not just reading what Aunty Miriam had written. I was really praying for God to help our priests and people to do his work in the church."

Her father had been listening to the conversation, although he appeared to be reading the newspaper. He came in quietly and gave Christina a big hug, saying, "God, I thank you for my little girl who is learning to love you and to have faith in you. I am so proud of you little one."

Samuel leapt onto his father's back as he bent over to hug Christina singing "I have grown too Daddy, I have faith in God. Christina and I always talk about Jesus and how He is our friend and how He will help our family. Sometimes Jason and Ron sit under the guava tree with us and we talk about Father Paul and some of the things he teaches us. Jason thinks he wants to be a priest. We really love our Church."

Mathew announced good news: "We are having pizza on the balcony tonight and guess what? Aunty Miriam wants to play 20 questions." "Oh great" said Samuel, "I am going to have some puzzles for all the grown-ups." "Are we ordering from the Pizza Parlour?" Christina asked. "Oh no, Grandma is making pizza with very interesting toppings," replied her Dad. "Like crab and shrimp?" Christina asked. "You know I only like cheese on my pizza," lamented Samuel.

"Do not worry," their Dad said reassuringly, "Grandma always thinks of what each person likes."

"Is Father Paul coming?" asked Samuel. "Of course not," his father replied. "It is Saturday evening and he has to prepare the Sunday Liturgy." "What is the Liturgy, Daddy?" Samuel asked as he was always curious about new words. "Let's see! I believe it means all the services and ceremonies of the Church. On Sundays and weekdays, for example, we celebrate the liturgy of the Eucharist," his Dad said. " I know what that means," said Samuel excitedly.

Christina remarked, "Father Paul always says that if you are not sure, you should check the Catechism of the Catholic Church. He said every Catholic home should have one. I told him we have two. Sr. Ryan gave one to Mummy for her birthday and Grandma Esther has a big one next to her bible on the shelf near her altar. I am going to get Mummy's. It is smaller and Mummy says it explains things well."

Christina liked to check things out to make sure she was correct. She hated being told that she was wrong. Out came the book. She checked the index as she had learned to do in school. "Page 126," she announced, "and here it is". "The Sacrament of the Eucharist is at the centre and heart of the Liturgy of the Catholic Church," she read, and remarked, "It has a long paragraph but it does not explain the word Liturgy. It has the Liturgy of the Word and the Liturgy of the Eucharist". "So what do you think Liturgy means?" her father asked gently. "I think it means a kind of ceremony," Christina replied.

"The readings for the day make up the Liturgy of the Word." her father explained. "And the Liturgy of the Eucharist, I am sure you understand. Your Grandmother is always talking about that." "It has a few long sections that explain everything Grandma is always telling us," Christina continued. "Perhaps we can read it at our devotions tomorrow evening." her father suggested.

Through all this Samuel was quiet, "I cannot read these big words," he complained. "Do not worry," Christina comforted him, "I will teach you." "Is the Eucharist a Sacrament?" Christina asked with a puzzled expression. Grandma expressed her consternation, "Miss Christina, what kind of question is that? You learnt about the seven Sacraments before you made your First Communion." "I know them, Grandma," shouted Samuel and he rattled them off: "Baptism, Confirmation, Holy Eucharist, Reconciliation, etc. etc.". "There are no sacraments called etcetera," Grandma chided. "I need to hear you both name them all before supper this evening. You do a good job and I will fix an extra pizza for you." They both ran off to Christina's room to get ready for the challenge.

However, distracted by their eagerness to challenge the adults with twenty questions later, they soon forgot their assigned task.

Samuel said," I really want us to win at Twenty Questions tonight. Let's play Twenty Questions about Church things. Let's practice." "Okay," Christina agreed, "you start."

Samuel—   "I am thinking of something. Remember you are allowed only twenty questions."

Christina— "Is it alive?"

Samuel—   "No."

Christina— "Is it made of stone?"

Samuel—   "No."

Christina— "Wood?"

Samuel—   "Yes."

Christina— "Is it a building?"

Samuel—   "No."

Christina— "Can you find it in a building?"

Samuel—   "Yes."

Christina— " In a house?"

Samuel—   "No."

Christina— "In a school?"

Samuel—   "No."

Christina— "In a Church?"

Samuel—   "Yes."

Christina—   "Does it begin with the letter 'A'?"

Samuel—   "Yes."

Christina—   "Is it an altar?"

Samuel—   "No."

Christina—   "How is it used in church?"

Samuel—   "Remember answers can only be 'yes' or ' no'."

Christina—   "Is it the table of the Eucharist?"

Samuel—   "No."

Christina—   "The lectern for the readings?"

Samuel—   "Yes, but you have to name it."

Christina—   "I can. It is an AMBO."

"Think we can try it on the adults?" Samuel asked. "I am not sure they know the word. Father Paul taught that at Mass last Sunday." Samuel continued." Father Paul said every Catholic Church has two tables—the Table of the Word, where the Liturgy of the Word is read and the Table of the Eucharist, where the gifts of bread and wine are changed into the Body and Blood of Christ."

"It is my turn now," Christina announced, "I think I have a puzzle. See if you get it."

Samuel— "Is it alive?"

Christina— "No."

Samuel— "Is it made of wood?"

Christina— "Yes."

Samuel— "Is it found in a home?"

Christina— "No."

Samuel— "Is it in a Church?"

Christina— "Yes."

Samuel— "It is not the Table of the Readings?"

Christina— "No."

Samuel— "Then it must be the confessional!"

Christina— "Yes."

"Samuel, boy, you are so smart. I did not think you would get it. I love my little brother," exclaimed Christina. Samuel was beaming with pride. "So," Christina asked, "What is a confessional?" "Okay." Samuel cocked his head to one side as he always did when he was cocksure of an answer. "It is that small room at the back of the Church where you receive the Sacrament of Reconciliation."

"Wow! You are good!" Christina said. "And what is the Sacrament of Reconciliation, little boy?" Christina asked. "You confess your sins and the priest forgives you in the name of Jesus, just as he has the power to change bread and wine into the Body and Blood of Christ," Samuel replied, beaming from ear to ear. Christina continued in her adult manner, "His anointing also gives him the power to forgive sins just as Jesus did."

"Now let me see if I can get all the names of the Sacraments in the Catechism, before Grandma call us for dinner." Christina went through the index. "Page 121," she announced and so they learnt the names so Grandma would be proud of them. "Baptism, Confirmation, Holy Eucharist, Reconciliation, Holy Orders, Matrimony, Anointing of the Sick". Christina said, "We will do it like that—when Grandma asks, say one and I will say another so together we will have it all covered."

At supper that evening Aunty Miriam gleefully announced "And now 20 Questions and I start". Both Christina and Samuel begged at once, "Please can we start?" Aunty Miriam gave in. Then Christina and Samuel tried the 'AMBO' and 'confessional.' The adults had not known that the table of the Liturgy of the Word was called the AMBO.

"There is so much to learn about our church," Grandma Esther remarked. "I am 80 and still learning. At Holy Mass, I follow the liturgy so closely. When Father gives the final blessing, I feel ready to face the world. We confess, we listen to the Word, we offer our gifts and we share in Communion; we give thanks and we receive the blessing. Our service is a wonderful expression of our love and trust in God and His care for us. This is why I am a Catholic!" she announced proudly.

CHAPTER 10

BLESSINGS

It was an exciting yet sad day. The children and their parents were returning to the city. That left Grandma Esther alone in Cedarville. She was sad; she would miss her grandchildren. The last thirteen weeks were so full of fun and excitement but Grandma Esther was also content and at peace.

Life was almost normal again in the Emmanuel household. Samuel, like Jason, wanted to be an acolyte to serve at Holy Mass and other church events. He was going to see the acolyte leader on Saturday. Christina was returning to her Confirmation class and she was eager to give an account of her time in Cedarville, to tell her class specifically what she had learnt about the Eucharist.

Now Matthew was at home with his entire family—Ruth, Christina and Samuel. You could see pride welling up in him as he prepared to pray before the evening meal. The family sat at the table holding hands. Their father asked them all to bow their heads. He said the Grace and then lifted his head, looked around at his family and said, "I want to say something about today's reflection in the 'Living Faith.'" The children looked at each other, mildly surprised and their mom smiled. Their father continued, "Your mother will read from John Chapter 6: 1-15. Christina sat up and stated confidently, "That is the story of the loaves and the two fish."

"How did you know?" her father asked. Christina smiled and explained, "Grandma Esther always said that John, Chapter 6, is very comforting. The apostle tells us how much Jesus loves and cares for us. He tells how Jesus can work miracles in our lives. Can we read together, Mummy? You read one verse and I will read the next, okay?" Everyone echoed "Okay."

At the end of the reading their Dad said softly, "I want you to remember Grandma Esther's words on this reading and remember that Jesus provides for us always. He provides food for our material needs and He provides food for our spiritual needs. The Eucharist will always sustain us no matter what we are going through. By receiving Jesus often, we fill our lives with grace and power. We have to trust Him and He will provide all our needs. We see that in His time with His disciples. He loved them very much and always came to their rescue when they were in difficult situations. Do you remember what happened when Jesus walked on the water and invited Peter to join Him?" Samuel said, "Yes, I remember. Peter almost drowned." Everyone laughed.

Their Dad replied, "Yes, that is because Peter became afraid and lost his trust in Jesus. When we lose trust in God, things always go wrong." Christina leapt up and said, "That sounds like Grandma Esther's favourite saying, 'When things get tough, a silent prayer is enough.'"

Her mother replied, "Yes, that is true. Sometimes when things go wrong, we should not give up, but say a prayer and trust in God who will see us through. Let's continue with our meal." Christina remarked," This pasta tastes really good but not as great as Grandma Esther's." "It will still make your stomach happy," her mother replied. "Oh no," Christina said "Your stomach gets happy only after you receive Holy Communion and this is only dinner."

"Okay," said Matthew, "do not get confused. Pasta fills our stomach and strengthens the body. Our stomach feels happy also when it is filled with food. However, the Eucharist is food for our soul and nothing else can satisfy the soul but the Eucharist. Holy Communion makes Grandma Esther's stomach happy because she believes that nothing else can satisfy the soul except the Body and Blood of Jesus Christ. For Catholics, this teaching is the core of our faith."

"Daddy, what do you mean by core?" asked Samuel. Matthew replied, "It means that the Eucharist is the centre of our Catholic faith because the Eucharist is how we meet God on earth through Jesus." "That sounds like a big thing to understand," Samuel remarked.

"I have an idea,' Christina said thoughtfully. "Father Paul always asks us to check the Catechism book when we are unsure about these things. Mummy's small one explains things well." She dashed out of the room and returned with the book, announcing loudly "once again page 126 — now listen Samuel. It says: "The Sacrament of the Eucharist is the centre and Heart of the Liturgy of the Catholic Church for in it she fulfills, day after day, all over the world, the command that Christ gave to his Apostles on the night before He suffered, when he said: 'Do this in memory of Me' and so our celebration is rooted in the commemoration of the Last Supper of Jesus.' So 'root' and 'core' and 'centre' all mean the same thing." Christina continued to explain, " take a plant as an example; the root is the life centre of the plant. If we do not nurture the root, the plant dies. So too, the Eucharist is the root or core of our spiritual life. If we neglect the Eucharist, our spiritual life dies." Matthew and Ruth smiled at each other. Christina was getting so mature and they felt really proud.

Samuel was very pensive and asked slowly, "Soooo, how do we keep Jesus alive in our hearts?" "Food for the soul—Holy Communion, Christina answered. "You remember Grandma goes to Mass everyday and always comes home singing 'I am the Bread of Life'."

"Do we really die?" Samuel asked anxiously. Ruth said, "Come here son," and she hugged him explaining, "This is what I was saying earlier. Pasta feeds our body. Holy Communion feeds our soul. We have to try to be strong in body and soul if we are to live good lives. Grandma Esther has taught us how to do both. We must never forget these lessons as long as we live."

Appendix A

Glossary (a) Liturgical

Acolyte:

A person who helps the priest when he performs religious duties during Mass or religious ceremonies.

The acolytes accompany the priest at the entrance procession.

Adoration:

To worship and show a deep love for God.

We kneel and bow before the altar in adoration of the Blessed Sacrament.

Ambo:

The lectern where the readings and gospel of the day are read by the lectors and celebrant of the Mass: the place where the Word is proclaimed.

The celebrant of the Mass proclaimed the gospel of the day and delivered the teaching at the ambo.

Catechism:

Instruction given in questions and answers on matters of the Catholic Faith.

Our instructions of Catechism come from the book "Catechism of the Catholic Church", which we must learn and study.

Chalice:

The cup in which the wine is poured for the Consecration.

The priest or deacon pours the wine in the chalice before the Consecration.

Commemoration:

Remembering some person, place, thing or occasion with great honour and sacred celebration.

The mass was in commemoration of Grandma's eightieth birthday.

Congregation:

A group of persons coming together especially to praise and honour God.

The congregation stood up to sing the hymn.

Consecration:

The moment when the priest says the words which change the bread and wine into the Body and Blood of Jesus.

The boys were very quiet and reverent at Consecration.

Covenant:

An agreement between God and us.

The ten commandments are a covenant between God and His People.

Eucharist:

A Sacrament and a thanksgiving.

The Eucharist is the greatest form of thanksgiving we can offer God.

Faith:

Believing something without proof that it is true.

It is only by faith that we can accept the changing of bread and wine into the Body and Blood of Christ.

Holy Orders:

A sacrament bestowed on persons such as Bishops, Priests and Deacons set apart for ministry in the Church.

Father Paul received the Sacrament of Holy Orders at his ordination.

Homily:

Sermon or explanation of the Gospel readings.

In the homily the Priest presents the message of the readings in a way that the congregation can understand

Miracle:

An event which is remarkable but cannot be explained.

At the wedding feast in Cana Jesus performed his first miracle by turning water into wine to save the host from embarrassment.

Monstrance:

A receptacle used in the Roman Catholic Church to display the consecrated Eucharistic Host.

At the adoration service of Benediction, the priest blesses the congregation with the Eucharist displayed in the monstrance.

Mystery:

Something that is difficult or impossible to understand or explain.

The life of Jesus, especially the Passion, the Resurrection and the changing of the bread and wine into the Body and blood of Christ remains a mystery.

New Testament:

The twenty-seven books of the Bible written by the sacred authors in apostolic times which present Jesus Christ, His life, teaching and the beginnings of His church.

At catechism classes stories from the New Testament on the life of Jesus and the first Christians are taught.

Old Testament:

The Old Testament is a Christian term for a collection of religious writings by ancient Israelites that form the first section of Christian Bibles.

The Children surrounded their parent's bed to listen to stories from the book of the Old Testament. These stories tell of the creation of Adam and Eve; the Fall of Man; Cain and Abel; Noah and the flood; God's covenant with Abraham and Joseph and his brothers.

Offertory:

The principal part of the Mass in which the unconsecrated bread and wine are offered to God.

At the weekend masses members of the congregation are asked to participate in the offertory of the bread and wine before the consecration.

Ordination:

An admission to church ministry or conferrring of Holy Orders

A deacon receives some of the rites of a priest at his ordination.

Passover:

A Jewish festival commemorating the liberation of the Israelities from Egyptian bondage.

Jesus entered Jerusalem riding a donkey on His way to the Passover feast.

Proclaim:

To make known or to announce an action

During the Offertory at Mass, the priest proclaims the words of Consecration which change the bread and wine into the Body and Blood of Christ.

Prostrate:

Lying with face to the ground as a sign of submission.

During an ordination ceremony the candidate must prostrate before the altar as a sign of humbly accepting his responsibility as a priest.

Sacrament:

A sacrament is a special grace which we receive at different stages of our Christian life.

The Bishop or priest performs a special ceremony and through the power of the Holy Spirit we receive a very special grace.

There are seven sacraments—they are Baptism, Reconciliation, Holy Eucharist, Confirmation, Holy Orders, Matrimony and Anointing of the Sick.

Sacrifice:

To give up something in order to gain something valuable.

Jesus gave up His Life by dying on the cross as a sacrifice so that we could gain salvation.

Symbols:

A symbol is something that stands for or reminds us of something else .

There are many symbols in our church. The cross is a symbol that reminds us of the sacrifice that Christ made so that we could be saved and enter Heaven.

Synagogue:

A building where Jewish people meet for religious services.

There is a synagogue near the city of Bridgetown in Barbados.

Vestments:

The outer garments which the Bishop, priest and deacon wear for the celebration of Mass other church services.

At Easter members of the clergy wear white vestments.

Glossary (b) General

Admonished:

To give a warning; correcting a person kindly.

The teacher admonished the pupil and so prevented a fight.

Aroma:

Very fragrant smell; sweet smell, especially of food.

The aromas coming from Grandma Esther's kitchen made us feel very hungry.

Beckoned:

To attract attention by a movement of the hand or arm

With a sweeping wave of the arm we were beckoned to the lunch table.

Blurted:

To speak suddenly without thinking, sometimes of how the other will feel.

As the friend appeared in a new hairstyle the others blurted "Nice! Nice!"

Carmelite Community:

A religious order of ladies (nuns) who live and share life as sisters to each other

The nuns of the Carmelite Community take care of the elderly at the Marian Home in Saint Lucia.

Compliment:

An expression of praise.

The dancer was delighted to receive such a compliment.

Contagious:

To infect or communicate by contact

Measles is a highly contagious disease.

Crucified:

To put to death by nailing hands and feet to a cross.

Many early Christians were crucified for their faith.

Decaying:

Rotting

Since Lazarus had been dead for a few days, his body was disintegrating and rotting

Defiant:

Bold resistance or opposition to authority.

Christina was upset with her grandmother for objecting to the dress she wanted to wear and answered her defiantly

Dignified:

Showing pride and dignity.

Grandma was well dressed and walked with pride and dignity to Church to serve her God.

Eerie:

Weird or scary

Whenever there is a little light in a dark room, for example the light from a Virgin Lamp, shadows appear which can be scary

Excruciating:

Extremely painful and agonizing, causing intense suffering.

Christina had an excruciating headache, so she decided to take a rest.

Fragments:

A part broken off or detached

The saucer that Samuel broke lay in fragments on the kitchen floor.

Gracious:

To be courteous, kind and pleasant

Grandma Esther is the most gracious, helpful and generous lady in the community.

Harmonious:

Living in peace and friendship.

We hope that all immigrants can integrate and become harmonious after they've settled in the Saint Lucian society.

Hovered:

Stay in one place in the air or to hang fluttering or suspended.

A Jacquot hovered in the air, waiting to swoop down on its prey.

Pensive:

To be deep in sorrowful thought.

Mother looked pensive after she heard the news of the accident.

Instituted:

To establish, to bring into being.

Jesus instituted the sacrament of the Holy Eucharist at the last supper with his Apostles.

Interjected:

To intervene abruptly.

Christina interjected with the answer to the question which her dad had asked Samuel.

Jerusalem:

A holy city in Israel.

As Jesus entered Jerusalem on His way to the Passover feast the bystanders lined His way with palm branches.

Lamented:

To express sorrow or grief about something or some situation.

Martha and Mary's friends lamented at the death of their brother, Lazarus.

Lectern:

The stand from which the scripture lessons and also the gospel are read during a church service. It is also known as the Ambo.

The priest often uses the lectern to deliver his homily.

Majestically:

Very beautiful and stately, like a queen or a king.

The mountains stood majestically against the sky.

Metre:

A unit of measurement in the metric system

The rope was ten metres long.

Moor:

Moor can be used as a noun as well as a verb.

Moor (n) a large open grassy place

Moor (v) to keep a boat steady by attaching its rope to an anchor in order to bring it to shore.

As the fishermen approached the shore, the children helped to moor the boat.

Orphans:

Children whose parents have died.

Two of my friends in grade four are orphans; they live with their aunt.

Plateau:

An area high above the ground, where the land is flat and level.

The children loved to spend Easter vacation on the plateau at Cedarville with their grandmother.

Punctual:

To be on time.

The boys got a prize for always being punctual for class.

Quench:

To satisfy when you are thirsty.

We knew the cool orange drink would quench our thirst

Quizzically:

To show that you are puzzled or unsure.

The girls looked quizzically at the boys riding the horses into the churchyard.

Reassuringly:

To speak in a calm, confident and patient manner.

Their parents spoke reassuringly about their future in Cedarville.

Reel:

To pull something attached to a line on a spool, such as a fish.

Samuel wanted to help the fishermen reel in the fish.

Resist:

To avoid doing something which is tempting but wrong.

It is important to resist the influence of those who want us to do the wrong thing.

Significant:

Important.

The Consecration is the most significant part of the Mass

Sternly:

To speak in a very strict and serious tone.

Grandma spoke very sternly about behaving respectfully at Mass.

Sympathize:

To express support for someone who is grieving or going through a difficult time.

After Ron's accident the children went to visit and sympathize with his parents.

Symphony:

A harmonious blending of sounds.

The junior music band treated the crowd to a wonderful symphony.

Traditional:

Referring to things that were done in the past and continue to be done in the present.

It is traditional *to wear our National Dress on special occasions.*

Transformed:

To change the quality or essence of something.

The bread and wine are transformed at Consecration

Vibrant:

Bright and lively.

The warm sunshine on the green plants and flowers create vibrant colours on the plateau at Cedarville.

Appendix B

Discussion Questions

Chapter 1

1. Describe your favourite place of peace and quiet where you can think of God.

2. Describe your relationship with God.

3. Try to remember the first time you started feeling close to God and write about it.

4. Prayer is about talking to God. Explain a situation in which you or someone you know prayed and the prayers were answered.

5. Explain how God shows us His love.

Chapter 2

Read the hymn, 'I am the Bread of Life.' It is found in Moments of Celebration

No 148. Write down your thoughts about it as you pick out the part that you feel is most interesting.

Chapter 3

1. Have you ever seen a picture of the Last Supper? Carefully study the picture and write down what you observe.

2. What do you think people should do when they return to their seats after receiving Holy Communion? Think about this carefully. Give your reason (s).

Chapter 4

1. Have you ever witnessed an Ordination? If not, do some research. During the ceremony, the candidate prostrates or lies down on the floor before the altar. Why do think he does that?

2. Name the different colours of the vestments that the priest wears during the year. At Pentecost he wears red. Find out why the colours of his vestments change at different times.

Chapter 5

1. In this chapter there are many interesting and important words. Some of these are listed below. Find out what each means and prepare to explain the meaning of each to anyone who might ask you : Anointing, covenant, proclaims, Eucharist, renew, Divine, faith, pensive, hovered, prostrate.

2. In this chapter we read that the Offertory and Consecration are important parts of the Mass. Find out all the parts of the Mass and write them down in the correct order.

3. What do you understand by the saying, "Faith can move mountains ?"

    (see Matthew Chapter 17 Verse 20)

4. Faith means believing something even though you cannot explain it. Discuss some of the teachings of your church that you accept by faith.

Chapter 6

1. What do you understand by the word neighbour? Describe ways in which you can be good to your neighbour.

2. On which Sunday do we remember the time that Jesus rode into Jerusalem and the people were shouting, "Blessed is He who cometh in the name of the Lord. Hosanna in the Highest?"

Name some of the hymns that are sung on that special Sunday.

3. What name was given to the twelve special friends who followed Jesus? Give the name of each of them.

4. Not all of the twelve, who were with Jesus, wrote the Gospels. Give the names of those who wrote the gospels and indicate which ones among them were apostles.

5. Do you know that Jews still celebrate the Passover? Find out what it is.

Chapter 7

1. Imagine you are talking to a group of non—Catholics. Explain fully to them what happens at Consecration.

2. In the story we read that Samuel did not understand the mystery of Holy Communion. Do you know what the word 'mystery' means? Find out other mysteries in Catholic teaching.

3. Give the details of the first miracle that Jesus performed?

Chapter 8

1. In this chapter, we read about giving thanks. Just pause for a moment and think of all that you are thankful for. Write or say a short prayer of thanksgiving.

2. Do you know that Jesus Himself taught that it is important to say thanks? In the Bible we read a story about something wonderful that He did for ten people. Of these, only one returned to say thanks. He did not like this and He asked the question, "Where are the other nine?" Read the story for yourself.

3. At parties we normally have lots to eat and drink. Do you know that in some countries there are times when people go hungry for many days? Find out the different reasons why people sometimes go hungry for a long time.

4. What is the name given to the period when there is no rain and plants dry up and die? Give the name of a condition/situation in which the crops dry up for such a long period that there is no food and people starve.

5. Grandma thought that the dress with the mini skirt and spaghetti straps was not suitable for Christina to wear to church. Give reasons why you agree or disagree with her. Suggest other outfits that some people might think are unsuitable for church. Design some outfits that you consider appropriate for church.

Chapter 9.

1. Do you play together as a family? Name one game that you play. If you do not, then try to introduce the practice. (You may use the one in this Chapter)

2. What are the benefits of playing games together as a family?

3. Let us use the power of your brains. Write a poem, a song or a paragraph about the Consecration.

ABOUT THE AUTHORS

Martha Isaac is a retired university lecturer. She is the author of the devotional ' Reclaiming our Citadel: Reflections on Widowhood. She serves as a catechist in her parish. She has two grown daughters and four grandchildren.

Emma Bernard-Joseph is a retired Administrative Professional Secretary, who currently works with the Saint Lucia Blind Welfare Association, a non-profit organisation working with and for blind and visually impaired persons. Mrs. Bernard-Joseph is an active member of the St. Benedict's Parish and is very involved in all matters of Parish life.

Martha Celestin began her career as a Primary School Teacher. In 1970 she became a secretary and after qualifying as an Administrative Professional Secretary, she held the position of Administrative Assistant to the Chairman and Managing Director of a shipping company until her retirement in 1994.

Julia Hennecart is a retired educator having served as principal of a Catholic Girl's school for a number of years. She also serves as an extraordinary minister of the Eucharist and also teaches confirmation students. She is mother of five and grandmother of ten.

Ingrid Millar has given 30 years of service to the Saint Lucia Tourist Board. She worked with at least seven Directors of Tourism as Executive Secretary and now serves as Administrative Manager.

Ingrid enjoys photography and family moments with her husband and two sons.

Agatha Mortley-Modeste is a retired Educational Administrator. She devoted most of her years as a teacher to the teaching of English Language and English Literature. However, her early experience in teaching was as an infant School teacher. She is actively involved in social work in her parish. Agatha is married and has two grown children.

Esther Lubin—Stephen is a retired Elementary School Teacher. She taught all classes from kindergarten to standard six and beyond. She comes from a family of fourteen. Her own family consists of five children with the four remaining adults holding their own successfully in the communities where they currently reside.

She has a passion for cooking, gardening and family.

Editor - Loyola Devaux has recently retired after 45 years as a teacher. Her last twenty years were spent as a lecturer at Sir Arthur Lewis Community College in Communication Studies. She led an active life as Head of Department for over a decade as well as being involved in various areas of her church community and social work on a voluntary basis.

She is married and has five grown children and nine grandchildren .

Printed in the United States
By Bookmasters